To:

From:

Nevertheless,

She

Persisted

COMPILED BY THE PETER PAUPER PRESS EDITORS
WITH TESSLYN PANDARAKALAM

PETER PAUPER PRESS, INC.
WHITE PLAINS, NEW YORK

FOR WOMEN EVERYWHERE,
NEVER STOP TRYING. NEVER STOP BELIEVING.
NEVER GIVE UP.

Images used under license from
Shutterstock.com and Creative Market

Designed by Tesslyn Pandarakalam

14 13 12 11

"Nevertheless, she persisted" has become a rallying cry ever since Elizabeth Warren was silenced in the Senate in 2017. We will *not* sit down and be quiet. We will continue—with renewed vigor—to overcome obstacles on our path to power, both personal and political.

Whether you're fighting for a cause or becoming your own champion on the road to achieving your dreams, let this little treasury of empowering thoughts inspire your journey.

What I've learned is that real change is very, very hard. But I've also learned that change is possible—if you fight for it.

ELIZABETH WARREN

I RAISE UP MY VOICE—NOT SO THAT I CAN SHOUT, BUT SO THAT THOSE WITHOUT A VOICE CAN BE HEARD.

Malala Yousafzai

WE DO NOT NEED MAGIC TO
CHANGE THE WORLD.
WE CARRY ALL THE POWER
WE NEED INSIDE OURSELVES
ALREADY. WE HAVE THE POWER
TO IMAGINE BETTER.

J.K. Rowling

I did not really know what I wanted to do, but I did know the kind of woman I wanted to be. And I wanted to be an independent woman, a woman who is in the driving seat, and who is in charge of her own life.

Diane von Furstenberg

I'VE BEEN ABSOLUTELY TERRIFIED EVERY MOMENT OF MY LIFE— AND I'VE NEVER LET IT KEEP ME FROM DOING A SINGLE THING I WANTED TO DO.

Georgia OKeeffe

Success is not the absence of failure; it's the persistence through failure.

AISHA TYLER

Be your own artist, and always be confident in what you're doing. If you're not going to be confident, you might as well not be doing it.

ARETHA FRANKLIN

JUST DON'T GIVE UP
TRYING TO DO WHAT
YOU REALLY WANT TO
DO. WHERE THERE IS
LOVE AND INSPIRATION,
I DON'T THINK YOU CAN
GO WRONG.

ELLA FITZGERALD

Life sometimes brings
enormous difficulties and
challenges that seem just too hard
to bear. But bear them you can,
and bear them you will, and your
life can have a purpose.

Barbara Walters

GROUP CONFORMITY SCARES
THE PANTS OFF ME BECAUSE
IT'S SO OFTEN A PRELUDE TO
CRUELTY TOWARD ANYONE
WHO DOESN'T WANT TO—OR CAN'T—
JOIN THE BIG PARADE.

Bette Midler

I HOPE THAT I INSPIRE WOMEN
TO BELIEVE IN THEMSELVES,
NO MATTER WHERE THEY COME
FROM; NO MATTER WHAT
EDUCATION THEY HAVE; WHAT
PARTICULAR BACKGROUND
THEY ORIGINATE FROM.

Madonna

There is a special place in heaven for anyone who speaks truth to power.

MADELEINE ALBRIGHT

I have insecurities of course, but I don't hang out with anyone who points them out to me.

ADELE

ALWAYS WORK HARD
AND HAVE FUN IN WHAT
YOU DO BECAUSE I THINK
THAT'S WHEN YOU'RE
MORE SUCCESSFUL.
YOU HAVE TO CHOOSE
TO DO IT.

SIMONE BILES

WHAT YOU DO MAKES
A DIFFERENCE, AND YOU HAVE TO
DECIDE WHAT KIND OF DIFFERENCE
YOU WANT TO MAKE.

Jane Goodall

Organize, agitate, educate, must be our war cry.

Susan B. Anthony

THE ANSWER TO LIFE IS YES.
THIS IS THE ONLY LIFE YOU HAVE SO
MAKE THE MOST OF IT. TAKE EVERY
OPPORTUNITY AND RISK YOU CAN.
YOU'LL ONLY REGRET THE THINGS
YOU DIDN'T DO BECAUSE YOU WERE
AFRAID TO TRY.

Cecile Richards

Persistence is critical.
Being creative and
persistent is even better.
Be fearless. Have the
courage to take risks.
Go where there are no
guarantees. Get out of your
comfort zone, even if it
means being
uncomfortable.

KATIE COURIC

So keep moving forward. And don't be frustrated when your path gets messy because it will get messy. You'll fall and you'll fail along the way. Wildly. Embrace the mess. ... Get ready for it. And don't let the potential to fail stop you from moving forward.

Octavia Spencer

PERSEVERANCE IS FAILING 19 TIMES AND SUCCEEDING THE 20TH.

Julie Andrews

THERE'S NO SUBSTITUTE
FOR SELF-RESPECT,
BANDING TOGETHER
WITH OTHER PEOPLE,
STANDING UP FOR
OURSELVES. LIBERATION
DOES NOT COME FROM
OUTSIDE. POWER CAN'T BE
GIVEN TO YOU. THE PROCESS OF
TAKING IT IS PART OF
THE EMPOWERMENT.

GLORIA STEINEM

It's our challenges and obstacles
that give us layers of depth and
make us interesting. Are they fun
when they happen? No. But they
are what make us unique.

ELLEN DEGENERES

We may encounter many defeats, but we must not be defeated.

MAYA ANGELOU

BEWARE, FOR I AM FEARLESS AND THEREFORE POWERFUL.

Mary Shelley

CHARACTER CANNOT BE
DEVELOPED IN EASE AND
QUIET. ONLY THROUGH
EXPERIENCE OF TRIAL AND
SUFFERING CAN THE SOUL
BE STRENGTHENED,
VISION CLEARED,
AMBITION INSPIRED, AND
SUCCESS ACHIEVED.

Helen Keller

This journey has always been about reaching your own other shore no matter what it is, and that dream continues.

Diana Nyad

In every position I've been in, there have always been naysayers who don't believe I'm qualified or who don't believe I can do the work. And I feel a special responsibility to prove them wrong.

Justice Sonia Sotomayor

Women have to harness their power—it's absolutely true. It's just learning not to take the first no. And if you can't go straight ahead, you go around the corner.

CHER

You should never view your challenges as a disadvantage. Instead, it's important for you to understand that your experience facing and overcoming adversity is actually one of your biggest advantages.

MICHELLE OBAMA

DITCH THE DREAM AND BE A DOER, NOT A DREAMER. MAYBE YOU KNOW EXACTLY WHAT IT IS YOU DREAM OF BEING, OR MAYBE YOU'RE PARALYZED BECAUSE YOU HAVE NO IDEA WHAT YOUR PASSION IS. THE TRUTH IS, IT DOESN'T MATTER. YOU DON'T HAVE TO KNOW. YOU JUST HAVE TO KEEP MOVING FORWARD. YOU JUST HAVE TO KEEP DOING SOMETHING, SEIZING THE NEXT OPPORTUNITY, STAYING OPEN TO TRYING SOMETHING NEW.

SHONDA RHIMES

Woman must
not accept;
she must
challenge.

MargaretSanger

YOUR PASSION MAY BE HARD TO
SPOT, SO KEEP AN OPEN MIND AND
KEEP SEARCHING. AND WHEN YOU
FIND YOUR PASSION, IT IS YOURS,
NOT WHAT SOMEONE ELSE THINKS
IT SHOULD BE. DON'T LET ANYONE
ELSE DEFINE YOUR PASSION FOR
YOU BECAUSE OF YOUR GENDER OR
THE COLOR OF YOUR SKIN.

Condoleezza Rice

I CAN NEVER BE SAFE;
I ALWAYS TRY AND GO
AGAINST THE GRAIN. AS
SOON AS I ACCOMPLISH
ONE THING, I JUST SET
A HIGHER GOAL. THAT'S
HOW I'VE GOTTEN TO
WHERE I AM.

BEYONCÉ

Don't let your fears overwhelm your desire. Let the barriers you face—and there will be barriers—be external, not internal. Fortune does favor the bold, and I promise that you will never know what you're capable of unless you try.

SHERYL SANDBERG

Opportunities are not offered. They must be wrested and worked for. And this calls for perseverance... and courage.

INDIRA GANDHI

GO TO FIND COMMON
GROUND; WHERE YOU
CAN'T, YOU STAND
YOUR GROUND.

NANCY PELOSI

SUCCESS DOESN'T
COME TO YOU —
YOU GO TO IT.

Marva Collins

Whatever you choose, however many roads you travel, I hope that you choose not to be a lady. I hope you will find some way to break the rules and make a little trouble out there. And I also hope that you will choose to make some of that trouble on behalf of women.

Nora Ephron

EVERY GREAT DREAM BEGINS
WITH A DREAMER. ALWAYS
REMEMBER, YOU HAVE WITHIN
YOU THE STRENGTH, THE
PATIENCE, AND THE PASSION
TO REACH FOR THE STARS TO
CHANGE THE WORLD.

Harriet Tubman

Women have begun to see
that if I go through that
doorway, I take everybody
through it.

Dianne Feinstein

You have to
participate
relentlessly in the
manifestations of
your own blessings.

ELIZABETH GILBERT

WHEN I BELIEVE IN SOMETHING, I'M LIKE A DOG WITH A BONE.

MELISSA MCCARTHY

YOU MAY HAVE
TO FIGHT A
BATTLE MORE
THAN ONCE TO
WIN IT.

Margaret Thatcher

Integrate what you believe in every single area of your life. Take your heart to work and ask the most and best of everybody else, too.

MERYL STREEP

I WILL NOT HAVE MY LIFE NARROWED DOWN. I WILL NOT BOW DOWN TO SOMEBODY ELSE'S WHIM OR TO SOMEONE ELSE'S IGNORANCE.

bell hooks

The secret of our success is that we never, never give up.

WILMA MANKILLER

IT'S GOOD TO DO UNCOMFORTABLE THINGS. IT'S WEIGHT TRAINING FOR LIFE.

AnneLamott

"I CAN'T" ARE TWO WORDS
THAT HAVE NEVER BEEN
IN MY VOCABULARY. I BELIEVE
IN ME MORE THAN ANYTHING
IN THIS WORLD.

Wilma Rudolph

Think like a queen.
A queen is not afraid
to fail. Failure is
another stepping-
stone to greatness.

OPRAH WINFREY

MAKE THE MOST OF
YOURSELF BY FANNING
THE TINY, INNER SPARKS
OF POSSIBILITY INTO
FLAMES OF ACHIEVEMENT.

GOLDA MEIR

KNOWING
WHAT MUST BE
DONE DOES
AWAY WITH FEAR.

ROSA PARKS

FEARLESSNESS MAY BE A GIFT BUT
PERHAPS MORE PRECIOUS IS THE COURAGE
ACQUIRED THROUGH ENDEAVOR,
COURAGE THAT COMES FROM
CULTIVATING THE HABIT OF REFUSING
TO LET FEAR DICTATE ONE'S ACTIONS,
COURAGE THAT COULD BE DESCRIBED AS
"GRACE UNDER PRESSURE"—GRACE WHICH
IS RENEWED REPEATEDLY IN THE FACE OF
HARSH, UNREMITTING PRESSURE.

AUNG SAN SUU KYI

WHEN YOU
GET INTO A TIGHT
PLACE AND EVERYTHING
GOES AGAINST YOU ...
NEVER GIVE UP THEN,
FOR THAT IS JUST THE
PLACE AND TIME WHEN
THE TIDE WILL TURN.

Harriet Beecher Stowe

Hold your head and your standards high even as people or circumstances try to pull you down.

TORY JOHNSON

JUST REMEMBER, YOU CAN DO ANY-
THING YOU SET YOUR MIND TO, BUT
IT TAKES ACTION, PERSEVERANCE,
AND FACING YOUR FEARS.

GILLIAN ANDERSON

You have trust in what you think. If you splinter yourself and try to please everyone, you can't.

ANNIE LEIBOVITZ

TO BE GRITTY IS TO KEEP PUTTING
ONE FOOT IN FRONT OF THE OTHER.
TO BE GRITTY IS TO HOLD FAST TO
AN INTERESTING AND PURPOSEFUL
GOAL. TO BE GRITTY IS TO INVEST,
DAY AFTER WEEK AFTER YEAR,
IN CHALLENGING PRACTICE. TO BE
GRITTY IS TO FALL DOWN SEVEN
TIMES, AND RISE EIGHT.

ANGELA DUCKWORTH

AND THE TROUBLE IS, IF YOU DON'T RISK ANYTHING, YOU RISK MORE.

Erica Jong

Don't try to squeeze into a glass slipper. Instead, shatter the glass ceiling.

PRIYANKA CHOPRA

YOU DON'T MAKE PROGRESS BY
STANDING ON THE SIDELINES
WHIMPERING AND COMPLAINING.
YOU MAKE PROGRESS BY
IMPLEMENTING IDEAS.

Shirley Chisholm

I always wanted to be somebody. If I made it, it's half because I was game enough to take a lot of punishment along the way and half because there were a lot of people who cared enough to help me.

Althea Gibson

DON'T LIMIT YOURSELF.
MANY PEOPLE LIMIT
THEMSELVES TO WHAT
THEY THINK THEY CAN
DO. YOU CAN GO AS
FAR AS YOUR MIND
LETS YOU. WHAT YOU
BELIEVE, REMEMBER,
YOU CAN ACHIEVE.

Mary Kay Ash

Fight for the things that
you care about. But do it
in a way that will lead
others to join you.

Ruth Bader Ginsburg

Life is not easy for any of us. But what of that? We must have perseverance and, above all, confidence in ourselves. We must believe we are gifted for something and that this thing must be attained.

MARIE CURIE

ACCEPT YOUR LACK OF KNOWLEDGE, AND USE IT AS YOUR ASSET. IF YOUR REASONS ARE YOUR OWN, YOUR PATH, EVEN IF IT'S A STRANGE AND CLUMSY PATH, WILL BE WHOLLY YOURS, AND YOU WILL CONTROL THE REWARDS OF WHAT YOU DO BY MAKING YOUR INTERNAL LIFE FULFILLING.

NATALIE PORTMAN

COURAGE IS NOT
THE ABSENCE OF FEAR,
IT'S OVERCOMING IT.

Natalie Dormer

The best things come out of us
letting go and giving into our
passion—and to define ourselves
before other people start defining us.

Azar Nafisi

I REALLY THINK A
CHAMPION IS DEFINED
NOT BY THEIR WINS BUT
BY HOW THEY CAN RECOVER
WHEN THEY FALL.

Serena Williams

ENERGY—INDUSTRY—REFUSAL TO BE DISCOURAGED—A PREVAILING SENSE OF HUMOR: THESE ARE ESSENTIAL IN OUR LIVES. AN ATTITUDE THAT GOES BEYOND AMBITION INTO THE REALM OF THE SPIRITUAL, THE UNCHARITABLE; WHAT IN BOXING, AS PERHAPS IN OTHER SPORTS, IS CALLED "HEART" — THE INDEFINABLE CORE OF AN INDIVIDUAL THAT DECLARES I WILL NOT GIVE UP; I WILL PERSEVERE.

JOYCE CAROL OATES

THERE'S NOTHING LIKE OVERCOMING SOMETHING THAT SCARES YOU SO MUCH. NOTHING FEELS BETTER.

Laura Wilkinson

The most difficult thing is the decision to act. The rest is merely tenacity. The fears are paper tigers. You can do anything you decide to do. You can act to change and control your life and the procedure. The process is its own reward.

Amelia Earhart

You gain strength, courage, and confidence by every experience in which you really stop to look fear in the face.... You must do the thing you think you cannot do.

ELEANOR ROOSEVELT

IF YOU REALLY BELIEVE IN WHAT YOU'RE DOING, WORK HARD, TAKE NOTHING PERSONALLY, AND IF SOMETHING BLOCKS ONE ROUTE, FIND ANOTHER. NEVER GIVE UP.

Laurie Notaro

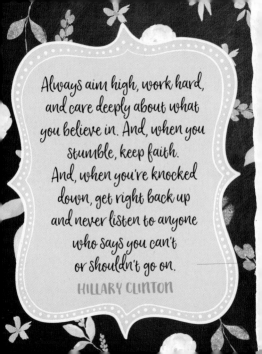

Always aim high, work hard, and care deeply about what you believe in. And, when you stumble, keep faith. And, when you're knocked down, get right back up and never listen to anyone who says you can't or shouldn't go on.

HILLARY CLINTON